Doing Justice, Showing Mercy

CHRISTIAN ACTION IN TODAY'S WORLD

13 Studies for Individuals or Groups

VINITA HAMPTON WRIGHT

SHAW

DOING JUSTICE, SHOWING MERCY
A SHAW BOOK
PUBLISHED BY WATERBROOK PRESS
5446 North Academy Boulevard, Suite 200
Colorado Springs, CO 80918
A division of Random House, Inc.

ISBN: 978-0-87788-180-3

146502721

CONTENTS

INTRODUCTION

"Justice" is a loaded word. It has been used by so many groups in the name of so many agendas that it is sometimes difficult to disassociate it from politics and militancy.

Yet a quick survey of Bible passages pertaining to justice will astound the most casual inquirer; once the reader has decided to take note of "justice," "oppression," and other related words, it becomes apparent that it is one of the key themes of both the Old and New Testaments. The reason for this is simple: as long as people, communities, and nations have existed, power has been abused, the poor have been neglected, and God has been grieved to the heart. His prophets cried out against fat and complacent ruling classes—often to their own persecution. Some of Jesus' strongest words were directed at those community leaders who exercised abusive power over the less educated, less wealthy, and less included.

"Mercy" is a different word altogether. We hardly hear it at all in day-to-day conversation. We associate it with softness, with people not "getting what they deserve." Discussions about law, order, and equality can go on for hours, but if a person were to introduce a question like, "What does it mean to be merciful?" he or she would likely be met with indignation or blank stares.

Many of the passages used for this study come from Old Testament law and prophecy. The laws of Exodus, Leviticus, Numbers, and Deuteronomy were applied during a time when God's people lived under God's rule alone—no king, no congress—in a political system called *theocracy*. It would be impractical to try and apply many of these laws in a literal sense to a society full of ethnic and religious differences and operating under newer political systems, such as democracy. But these laws have been given to us for a reason; they show us God's heart for fair and humane treatment—not only of people, but of animals and the environment. As we study these "law" passages, we will seek to discover God's desire for our behavior and principles for living in his kingdom.

Prophetic passages are set in specific times and situations but often carry larger meanings as well, such as the Old Testament passages that refer to the ministry of Jesus, centuries into the future. These segments also contain many references to historical events that were a part of Israel's history—events as familiar to their communities as George Washington crossing the Delaware and the signing of the Declaration of Independence are to Americans. It will be important for those using this study to pay attention to the Leader's Notes in order to understand the background to some of these passages.

God's message to humankind has always been double-edged: we have sinned and are cut off from God; yet God has forgiven us and made a way for us to return into fellowship. Likewise, God has always been grieved and angered at injustice in the world; yet the mercy shown throughout Bible events is really an *unbelievable,* even illogical mercy. If we are to have God's heart beating in us and live as citizens of the Kingdom of Heaven, we, too, must learn how to be just—and merciful.

HOW TO USE THIS STUDYGUIDE

Fisherman studyguides are based on the inductive approach to Bible study. Inductive study is discovery study; we discover what the Bible says as we ask questions about its content and search for answers. This is quite different from the process in which a teacher *tells* a group *about* the Bible and what it means and what to do about it. In inductive study God speaks directly to each of us through his Word.

A group functions best when a leader keeps the discussion on target, but this leader is neither the teacher nor the "answer person." A leader's responsibility is to *ask*—not *tell*. The answers come from the text itself as group members examine, discuss, and think together about the passage.

There are four kinds of questions in each study. The first is an *approach question*. Used before the Bible passage is read, this question breaks the ice and helps you focus on the topic of the Bible study. It begins to reveal where thoughts and feelings need to be transformed by Scripture.

Some of the earlier questions in each study are *observation questions* designed to help you find out basic facts—who, what, where, when, and how.

When you know what the Bible says you need to ask, *What does it mean?* These *interpretation questions* help you to discover the writer's basic message.

Application questions ask, *What does it mean to me?* They challenge you to live out the Scripture's life-transforming message.

Fisherman studyguides provide spaces between questions for jotting down responses and related questions you would like to raise in the group. Each group member should have a copy of the studyguide and may take a turn in leading the group.

A group should use any accurate, modern translation of the Bible such as the *New International Version,* the *New American Standard Bible,* the *Revised Standard Version,* the *New Jerusalem Bible,* or the *Good News Bible.* (Other translations or paraphrases of the Bible may be referred to when additional help is needed.) Bible commentaries should not be brought to a Bible study because they tend to dampen discussion and keep people from thinking for themselves.

SUGGESTIONS FOR GROUP LEADERS

1. Read and study the Bible passage thoroughly beforehand, grasping its themes and applying its teachings for yourself. Pray that the Holy Spirit will "guide you into truth" so that your leadership will guide others.

2. If the studyguide's questions ever seem ambiguous or unnatural to you, rephrase them, feeling free to add others that seem necessary to bring out the meaning of a verse.

3. Begin (and end) the study promptly. Start by asking someone to pray for God's help. Remember, the Holy Spirit is the teacher, not you!

4. Ask for volunteers to read the passages out loud.

5. As you ask the studyguide's questions in sequence, encourage everyone to participate in the discussion. If some are silent, ask, "What do you think, Heather?" or, "Dan, what can you add to that answer?" or suggest, "Let's have an answer from someone who hasn't spoken up yet."

6. If a question comes up that you can't answer, don't be afraid to admit that you're baffled! Assign the topic as a research project for someone to report on next week.

7. Keep the discussion moving and focused. Though tangents will inevitably be introduced, you can bring the discussion back to the topic at hand. Learn to pace the discussion so that you finish a study each session you meet.

8. Don't be afraid of silences: some questions take time to answer and some people need time to gather courage to speak. If silence persists, rephrase your question, but resist the temptation to answer it yourself.

9. If someone comes up with an answer that is clearly illogical or unbiblical, ask him or her for further clarification: "What verse suggests that to you?"

10. Discourage Bible-hopping and overuse of cross-references. Learn all you can from *this* passage, along with a few important references suggested in the studyguide.

11. Some questions are marked with a ♦. This indicates that further information is available in the Leader's Notes at the back of the guide.

12. For further information on getting a new Bible study group started and keeping it functioning effectively, read Gladys Hunt's *You Can Start a Bible Study Group* and *Pilgrims in Progress: Growing through Groups* by Jim and Carol Plueddemann.

SUGGESTIONS FOR GROUP MEMBERS

1. Learn and apply the following ground rules for effective Bible study. (If new members join the group later, review these guidelines with the whole group.)

2. Remember that your goal is to learn all that you can *from the Bible passage being studied.* Let it speak for itself without using Bible commentaries or other Bible passages. There is more than enough in each assigned passage to keep your group productively occupied for one session. Sticking to the passage saves the group from insecurity and confusion.

3. Avoid the temptation to bring up those fascinating tangents that don't really grow out of the passage you are discussing. If the topic is of common interest, you can bring it up later in informal conversation following the study. Meanwhile, help each other stick to the subject!

4. Encourage each other to participate. People remember best what they discover and verbalize for themselves. Some people are naturally shyer than others, or they may be afraid of making a mistake. If your discussion is free and friendly and you show real interest in what other group members think and feel, they will be more likely to speak up. Remember, the more people involved in a discussion, the richer it will be.

5. Guard yourself from answering too many questions or talking too much. Give others a chance to express themselves. If you are one who participates easily, discipline yourself by counting to ten before you open your mouth!

6. Make personal, honest applications and commit yourself to letting God's Word change you.

WHAT GOD REQUIRES
"to act justly"

Amos 5:11-15, 21-24; Jeremiah 22:11-17

He has showed you, O man, what is good.
And what does the LORD require of you?
To act justly and to love mercy
and to walk humbly with your God.
—*Micah 6:8*

"This is what the LORD Almighty says: 'Administer true justice; show mercy and compassion to one another. Do not oppress the widow or the fatherless, the alien or the poor. In your hearts do not think evil of each other.' "
—*Zechariah 7:9-10*

Amos is a "justice" book. The prophet was sent to deliver God's rebuke to the upper classes and political leaders of the northern kingdom of Israel. Much of their wealth had been generated by blatant oppression of the poor and the regular perversion of justice. In the chapters previous to this, Amos lambastes other surrounding kingdoms: Damascus, Gaza, Tyre, Edom, and so on. We can imagine the crowd gathering around the prophet and cheering as he pronounces judgment on the rival nations. But before long the sermon takes a rude turn, and the crowd no doubt grows silent, then angry, even abusive. For the denouncements are now falling on the nation Israel, and God seems to be even more upset with his own people—because they should know better, yet act as badly as those who worship idols.

1. If God were to send a prophet to America today, what five sins do you think the prophet would speak out against most loudly?

Read Amos 5:11-15.

2. What is the first offense mentioned in these verses?

What will be the immediate result of that offense?

3. It would seem obvious that God sees and knows all that is going on in the world. Why do you think the first part of verse 12 was included in this message to Israel?

4. *Oppression* is something that powerful people do to people who have less power. What does verse 12 imply about the standing of righteous people in that particular society?

In our present society, who is most often seen as "righteous" or good—people of influence (power) or people who have little or no voice in social affairs?

5. When the overriding atmosphere of a situation is evil, which people are often silenced (verse 13)?

♦ **6.** *Prudence* in the Bible refers to the act of gaining knowledge about a situation and of helping others to act wisely. Proverbs 22:3 says that "A prudent man sees danger and takes refuge . . ." *Righteous* refers to those who live rightly and justly. If the righteous people are being overpowered and the prudent people are not listened to, what do you think the results will be?

Do you see this happening in any situations today? At your school or work place? In the political arena? In matters of trade and economy? Give examples.

7. In verses 14-15 God gives instructions for maintaining a society that he will bless. There are three main parts to these instructions. What are they?

Wouldn't hating evil and loving good include maintaining "justice in the courts"? Why would God make special mention of it?

8. Look carefully at verse 14. Notice the very last phrase: "just as you say he is." What does this phrase indicate about the viewpoint of the people?

Read Amos 5:21-24.

9. What did the people rely on to gain God's favor?

What would be the equivalent activities in today's society?

10. What two things are desired by God more than any of the above?

How *much* justice and righteousness does God desire from us?

Read Jeremiah 22:11-17.

11. List the numerous sins referred to in this passage.

What has been the goal of the person described in these verses?

12. What does God say is the essence of a relationship with him (verse 16)?

Pretend that *you* are God's prophet. What are his priorities for your neighborhood? Your city or town? Your country?

FOR THOSE WHO LEAD

"woe to the shepherds"

Deuteronomy 17:14-20; Jeremiah 23:1-4, 16-18, 21-23; Matthew 23:1-28

"From the least to the greatest,
all are greedy for gain;
prophets and priests alike,
all practice deceit.
They dress the wound of my people
as though it were not serious.
'Peace, peace,' they say, when there is no peace."
—*Jeremiah 6:13-14*

"Their needs become our needs. Our shared needs then become the starting point of our ministry."—**John Perkins, *And Justice for All***

Jesus once said that to whom much is given, much will be required. And James warned people not to aspire to be teachers, because the greater responsibility meant greater accountability before God. Numerous Old Testament passages illustrate just how much God requires of those in leadership. Because a person of authority affects so many people, it is a serious offense to betray their trust. A leader sets the tone for living in his or her circle of influence—for good or for ill.

    1. Relate a situation in which a Christian leader led you or others—intentionally or not—in the wrong direction.

Read Deuteronomy 17:14-20.

◆   **2.** What is the king of Israel instructed *not* to do? What are the reasons for these restrictions?

    3. Why must the king read a copy of God's Law "all the days of his life" (verses 18-20)?

Read Jeremiah 23:1-4, 16-18, 21-23.

4. Who do you think is meant by "shepherds" in this passage?

Describe the kind of care the shepherds have given to their "sheep"—the people in their charge.

What is God's response?

♦ **5.** What was the duty of a prophet, as indicated by verses 16-18 and 21-22?

What are these "prophets" doing? What is the result of their prophecies?

6. What similarities do you see between "prophets" then and now?

Why must people in influential positions be very careful about saying, "The Lord told me . . ." or "God said . . . "?

Read Matthew 23:1-39.

7. Why does Jesus tell his listeners not to do what their teachers do? What do the teachers do (verses 4, 13, 23, 25, 37)?

8. What is the general motivation behind the teachers' actions (verse 5-7)?

9. These are among the strongest, most angry statements ever made by Jesus. Yet he saw sin at its worst day after day and was known for his compassion to the multitudes. Why do you think he is being so severe in this situation?

How do these teachers' actions affect those over whom they have authority (verses 4, 13, 23)?

10. Over whom do you have authority? Your children? Students? Coworkers? Have you ever abused that authority? In what way?

This week, spend time in prayer, asking the Holy Spirit to show you what your responsibilities are as a leader. Pray for help in being truthful and in putting others' needs before your own.

FOR THOSE WHO FOLLOW
"in repentance and rest"

Ezekiel 34:17-22; Isaiah 30:8-18; Matthew 25:31-46

"The prophets prophesy lies,
the priests rule by their own authority,
and my people love it this way. . . ."
—*Jeremiah 5:31*

The first half of Ezekiel 34 is a long indictment of Israel's leaders. They are likened to shepherds who only take care of themselves, leaving the sheep wounded, hungry, and without guidance. God says that he himself is going to take over the job: "I will shepherd the flock with justice."

But the judgment does not end with leaders. In the second half of that passage, Ezekiel the prophet delivers words of rebuke to the "sheep."

1. Time and again, some famous movie director will answer to the charge that sex and violence in films lead to

the degeneration of society's morals. The reply is always something like, "We only give the public what it wants. If it didn't sell, we wouldn't produce it." What is your opinion?

Read Ezekiel 34:17-22.

2. The prophet uses sheep as an illustration of how the people are treating one another. What actions and attitudes in today's society would be represented by verses 18-19? Verse 21?

3. What do you think is meant by God's statement that he "will judge between the fat sheep and the lean sheep"? What action is God going to take (verse 22)?

Read Isaiah 30:8-18.

4. What adjectives does God use to describe his people in verse 9? How have the people themselves affected the work of their leaders?

5. What do the people really want? What do they rely on?

6. What will the people's sin do to them? Can you see any of this happening today?

7. Where do we really find our salvation and strength?

Why could the people *not* have salvation and strength (verse 15)?

8. Where do we look for strength in hard times as a family? As a community? As a church? As a nation?

9. What does the Lord long to do (verse 18)?

Read Matthew 25:31-46.

10. List the similarities between this passage and the one in Ezekiel we just studied.

11. What makes the difference between sheep and goats in this teaching of Jesus?

When we help others, who else are we ministering to?

♦ **12.** What do we prove by our right treatment of others?

13. What attitudes, actions, and priorities in our general population contribute to the following problems?

overpriced goods in grocery stores
overflowing courtrooms
high divorce rate
money scandals
insufficient funds in social welfare programs
high dropout rate/low grade scores in public schools

This week, when you are tempted to blame government officials, your boss, or other people in authority for some problem, turn your complaint into a prayer for yourself, asking God to help you be a positive influence where you are.

THE PLACE OF POWER
"whoever wants to become great"

1 Kings 21; Mark 10:35-45

"Woe to those who plan iniquity,
to those who plot evil on their beds!
At morning's light they carry it out
because it is in their power to do it.
They covet fields and seize them,
and houses, and take them.
They defraud a man of his home,
a fellowman of his inheritance."
—*Micah 2:1-2*

"One measure of inequality . . . is the fact that, according to a United Nations survey of 83 countries, approximately three percent of all landlords have come to control almost 80 percent of the land. Another measure of inequality is the access to credit. In most countries only five to 20 percent of all producers have access to institutional credit.

The rest must turn to landlords and moneylenders at usurious rates running as high as 200 percent."—**Frances Moore Lappe & Joseph Collins,** *World Hunger: Ten Myths*

1. Think of someone you highly respect, someone for whom you would willingly do some task. Describe that person's character.

Now think of a person who has official authority over people but who is not respected. What are the character traits exhibited by him or her?

Read 1 Kings 21:1-16.

2. Judging from the first few verses of this story, what would you say was King Ahab's level of emotional maturity?

Why do people of great power and authority sometimes go unchecked in personal or ethical flaws?

♦ **3.** Why was Ahab's request for Naboth's property out of line?

4. What did Ahab's wife, Jezebel, do to alleviate the king's problem?

Why did Jezebel consider her actions justified (verse 7)?

5. How many parties were responsible for Naboth's death? List the people involved.

6. At what point could this plot have been stopped, or at least questioned (verse 11)?

7. What was Ahab's reaction when he learned that Naboth was dead?

Do you think Ahab suspected foul play? Why or why not?

Read 1 Kings 21:17-29.

8. Who did *God* hold responsible for Naboth's death (verse 19)?

Who was included in the punishment besides Ahab himself (verses 21-23)?

♦ **9.** What was Ahab's reaction when Elijah came to see
him?

Why had Elijah come to see Ahab (verse 20)?

♦ **10.** What was Elijah's message to Ahab?

What was the significance of dogs and birds eating the
remains of Ahab and Jezebel?

♦ **11.** How did Ahab respond to Elijah's message?

What was God's response to Ahab?

Read Mark 10:35-45.

12. What did James and John ask for?

In requesting these positions, what were James and John really wanting?

♦ **13.** How did Jesus respond to their request?

To what do you think he was referring in verse 38 when he used the terms "cup" and "baptism"?

14. Who does Jesus offer as an example of proper power and authority?

15. Have you ever been faced with expectations that would have you "lord it over" people rather than serve them? What did you do?

Make plans this month to serve the people over whom you have power.

WEALTH AND COMPLACENCY
"neither hot nor cold"

Amos 6:1-7; Ezekiel 16:49-50; Revelation 3:14-22

"There is something wrong with an ecclesiastical hierarchy which designates billions to build structures to honor One who said that he did not dwell in buildings made with hands. I am not convinced that God is all that honored by a church that puts up buildings for His glory while sacrificing comparatively little for those who cannot escape from grinding poverty."—**Tony Campolo,** *20 Hot Potatoes Christians Are Afraid to Touch*

Amos was a shepherd and keeper of fig trees in the southern kingdom of Judah. He was called by God to prophesy to the northern kingdom of Israel during the first half of the eighth century B.C. This was during the reign of Jeroboam II and the wealthiest period of Israel since the time of David and Solomon. It was also a time of great interest and participation in religion, with many well-attended rituals, holy days, and observances. But the people's religiosity kept them from seeing how needy they really were.

1. What to you would be a rich lifestyle? Is this different than a fulfilling lifestyle? Explain.

Read Amos 6:1-7.

2. What characteristics of the nation are named in verse 1?

What does the phrase "notable men of the foremost nation" imply?

3. Describe the lifestyle Amos is condemning. Why is it being judged so harshly?

What would be today's equivalents of the luxuries
described in these verses?

♦ **4.** This passage immediately follows the passage of Study
1, where the nation is condemned for its lack of justice
and the worship of idols (Amos 5:21-27). With this in
mind, what do you think is being "ruined" in the nation
(verse 6)?

What attitude does Amos say would be the appropriate
one for the people to have in this situation?

5. What does God promise will be the result of complacency?

During Amos' day, nations judged themselves on the basis of visible wealth and military power. In passages before and after this one there is frequent mention of idolatry, oppression of the poor, and arrogance. What not-so-visible qualities of a nation seem to claim God's priority?

Read Ezekiel 16:49-50.

6. The city of Sodom has been notorious throughout history for the sexual perversions practiced there. In this overview of wicked cities and their destructions, what sins are *specifically* named as the causes of Sodom's fall?

Read Revelation 3:14-22.

♦ **7.** Who is making the judgment in this passage?

8. What is the prevailing attitude of this church?

In what have its members placed their security?

9. What needs does Christ see?

What does he want to do for these people?

◆ **10.** What words of encouragement are offered in this passage?

11. What statements remind us of the responsibility we have before God (verses 20, 22)?

12. In what ways does your nation appear to be "great"—especially in the eyes of other nations? What do you think Amos would notice were he to make a visit?

Plan a time during the next week in which you can pray, asking the Holy Spirit what your real needs are. *During that time, set aside financial considerations altogether.* Ask God to help you see the needs of others, too.

DOWN WITH OPPRESSION!

"all the lands are at rest and peace"

Isaiah 14:3-17; James 5:1-6

"The LORD said, 'I have indeed seen the misery of my people in Egypt. I have heard them crying out because of their slave drivers, and I am concerned about their suffering. So I have come down to rescue them . . . and to bring them . . . into a good and spacious land . . . And now the cry of the Israelites has reached me, and I have seen the way the Egyptians are oppressing them. So now, go. I am sending you to Pharaoh to bring my people the Israelites out of Egypt.' "—*Exodus 3:7-10*

Most of us feel oppressed at one time or another. We use the word "oppressive" to describe the atmosphere in a room, someone with an overbearing personality, hostile politics in the workplace, or a military regime that commits atrocities against a specific group of people.

The kind of oppression covered by the passages of this study is considerably more serious than a person being passed over for a promotion or being billed unfairly by a shrewd auto mechanic. Isaiah and James are addressing the relentless and long-term abuse of people—individuals as well as entire nations.

1. Describe a situation in which you were treated wrongly or unfairly but were powerless to do anything about it.

Read Isaiah 14:3-8.

2. From what will God relieve his people?

♦ **3.** Think about a group of people you know who have been or are being kept in cruel bondage or forced to suffer. What kinds of turmoil are present in such an existence?

4. What will the Lord do to oppressors?

Describe how the oppressors treated the people (verse 6).

5. In the days of Isaiah oppression was often by physical and military means, and physical oppression is still present in many places. What are some more subtle ways in which oppressors vent their anger and "oppress relentlessly"?

♦ **6.** Verses 7-8 add an interesting angle to this subject. What else suffers under the hands of oppressors?

Read Isaiah 14:9-11.

7. What eventually happens to the powerful?

What events besides death show no respect for status?

Read Isaiah 14:12-17.

8. Many scholars view this passage as referring to Satan's fall from heaven. Whether Satan or a specific earthly ruler, what attitude caused the downfall of this oppressor who "made kingdoms tremble"?

If these verses do refer to Satan, then what do they reveal about his position? About his power?

Read James 5:1-6.

9. List the offenses of the people James is speaking against.

Which of these activities do you see in operation today? Give examples.

10. How can gold and silver be corroded? What would the corrosion indicate about the metal's quality in the first place?

What point do you think James is making about wealth in this life?

11. Is there any question that the rich will be in misery (verse 1)? Do we see this misery already, or does this prediction seem to be for the future only? Give evidence for your answer.

12. Do you think that being rich *in itself* brings God's condemnation, or do there seem to be conditions or actions that lead to such harsh judgment?

Are the rich always oppressors, and are oppressors always rich? Can you think of examples when the two do not go together—if so, what are they?

List several current oppressive situations that you know about. Try to think of neighborhood, national, and international examples. (For example, an abusive husband next door is oppressing his wife and children, a large company is taking advantage of migrant workers, a political regime is preventing food from reaching needy people.)

Pray specifically for those situations.

BALANCE OF WEALTH
"it shall be a jubilee"

Leviticus 25:8-38; Acts 6:1-7

"Our desire is not that others might be relieved while you are hard pressed, but that there might be equality. At the present time your plenty will supply what they need, so that in turn their plenty will supply what you need. Then there will be equality, as it is written: " 'He who gathered much did not have too much, and he who gathered little did not have too little.' "—*2 Corinthians 8:13-15*

In August of 1992, Hurricane Andrew left thousands of families homeless, without electricity and water during one of the year's hottest seasons. On top of the disaster itself came horrifying news reports of businesses selling electrical generators at the roadsides—at many times their ordinary price.

We are often shocked at how low some people will stoop in order to make a bigger profit. But God has always understood human selfishness. In Israel's early history, he set up laws and safeguards against the unfortunate being caught in a bottomless downward spiral, and against the rich building empires at others' expense.

1. What would it take to drastically change your financial situation for the worst?

Read Leviticus 25:8-38.

2. How often was the Year of Jubilee (verse 13)?

What was each person to do during that year (verses 10-12)?

3. On what basis were people to calculate the value of property (verses 14-17)? What was actually being sold (verse 16)?

4. Every fifty years, land was returned to the original family it belonged to. What business practices would this law curtail?

What was the justification behind such a "radical" practice (verse 23)?

♦ **5.** What effect would the Jubilee have on families who came upon hard times? On people who were very good at making money?

6. What practices were strictly forbidden concerning those who became poor (verses 36-38)?

7. What kinds of events in today's world can make the difference between a family being financially secure and being poor or even destitute?

Are some people more vulnerable to catastrophe than others? Who, and why? Who, if anyone, is exempt from financial ruin?

◆ **8.** What was the reward for following God's Jubilee instructions (verses 18-22)?

What kind of provisions did God promise for Israel's obedience?

♦ **9.** How would this system of land ownership—and, in essence, debt canceling—differ from communism? From capitalism?

How can the *principles* of this passage be applied in present economic systems?

Read Acts 6:1-7.

♦ **10.** What situation led to the need for deacons?

Was there ever a question that the widows should be provided for? What was the real problem?

11. Why would it be important that spiritually fit individuals look after such basic needs? What other issues are poor people often facing? What issues do the bereaved face that require more than merely material resources?

12. Who in your church community serves the needy? Is this considered a menial or a prestigious position?

Spend some time this week considering the subject of ownership. What is *yours*? What is *ours*? What is *private*? What is *community* property? What has shaped your attitudes about these definitions? Pray to arrive at a view that represents God's purposes for us.

OUR RESPONSE TO THE POOR
"remember that you were slaves"

Nehemiah 5:1-13; Deuteronomy 24:6, 10-15, 17-22

"You don't do any good putting on Band-Aids. You have to work continually with people. Band-Aids will help for a day, that's all."—**Mildred McWhorter,** director of three mission centers in Houston, *Christianity Today*

What causes poverty, anyway? Who is responsible for it? And what should we do about it? In these passages we see how practices of those with resources can affect those who have little. We receive instructions on how to show mercy and respect to people who are poor. And we are reminded of the real source of our wealth.

1. Think of a time when you didn't have the money that you needed. What kind of emotions did you experience? How did that period of want affect your outlook on life? If you've been fortunate enough not to have such an experience, try to imagine going through a period of illness with no savings account, credit cards, or other backup systems. Then, to top it off, your car needs a major repair. How do you feel?

Read Nehemiah 5:1-13.

2. What practices in Israel have led to excruciating poverty for many of its people? What natural disaster has contributed to the situation (verse 3)?

3. What are some families having to do merely to survive?

4. Famines were not unknown to Nehemiah; neither was poverty. What made him so angry about this situation?

Who did Nehemiah hold responsible for the state of affairs?

♦ **5.** Who had Jewish people sold themselves and their children to? Why was this especially horrible?

6. What other reason did Nehemiah declare for the Jewish leaders to act differently toward their own poor (verse 9)?

What were Nehemiah's orders (verses 10-11)?

7. What was wrong with charging interest in this situation?

Interest is so built into the present world financial system that we hardly think about it, except to determine between different interest rates. In light of this passage, under what circumstances would you consider doing away with interest on the loans you give?

Read Deuteronomy 24:6, 10-15, 17-22.

8. Why were creditors not allowed to take millstones as security for loans?

Why were creditors forbidden to keep a poor person's coat as collateral overnight?

When was an employer to pay workers who were poor?

◆ **9.** What was God's concern that is so poignantly demonstrated in verses 10-11? What need is God attending to by this command?

◆ **10.** What three categories of people were Israelites expressly forbidden to take advantage of (verses 17-18)? In what ways would these people be especially vulnerable?

11. What bit of important history does God use to help Israel keep a balanced perspective?

What might God use to keep *your* perspective in balance?

♦ **12.** How did the reaping practices described in verses 19-21 provide for the physical needs of the alien, fatherless, and widow? How were the mental/emotional needs provided for by this practice?

This week, write down

(1) Ways in which you can help the poor

(2) Ways in which you can help foreigners living here

(3) Ways in which you can help the poor help themselves, as in Deuteronomy 24:19-21

WHY CHRIST CAME
"by his wounds we are healed"

Isaiah 42:1-4; Luke 4:14-21; Isaiah 52:13–53:12

"On one side are evangelistic ministries—the 'soul-winners,' criticized for being concerned only with passing out tracts and making altar calls. On the other side are 'justice ministries,' whose critics say they are concerned more about ladling soup than giving out the Bread of Life.

"Meanwhile, the late-twentieth century world darkens daily, proof that such fragmenting of what the Lord requires of His people cripples our witness and makes widespread Christian impact in our culture impossible."
—**Charles Colson, "Doing Justice, Loving Mercy, Walking Humbly,"** *Discipleship Journal*

What does Christ's life, death, and resurrection have to do with justice? Didn't he come to save us from our sins, so that we can go to heaven when we die? Sometimes we allow that salvation message to overshadow other meanings of Jesus' life. Not only was Jesus concerned with justice in the here and now, his role in bringing it about was predicted centuries before his coming.

1. As a Christian, what hope do you have in an unjust world?

Read Isaiah 42:1-4.

2. What are the two titles given to the person talked about in these verses?

What do these titles mean to you?

3. What will this person do?

What will this person *not* do?

4. Look closely at verse 2. How is God's chosen one different from the usual type of revolutionary?

◆ **5.** What do you think these phrases mean, and why?:

"a bruised reed he will not break"

"a smoldering wick he will not snuff out"

What kind of attitude or character quality is implied by these phrases?

6. What makes it possible for this person to bring justice to the nations (verse 1)?

Why should a Christian today try to bring about justice in the world? What does the Christian have in common with the chosen one?

7. How determined is the chosen one in establishing justice?

What kinds of things discourage you, or make you falter in your attempts to live out your faith?

Read Luke 4:14-21.

♦ **8.** This is a passage from Isaiah 61:1-2 that Jesus has claimed as his purpose in life. What are his specific goals?

How is he able to accomplish them (verse 18)?

9. What is the good news (verse 18)?

Read Isaiah 52:13–53:12.

10. List all the ways in which this servant is like the oppressed, the poor, and the hurting.

How is his suffering *different* from our suffering?

11. What will God's servant accomplish by *his* suffering (53:10-12)?

12. What do Christ's life and death mean to people who are abused by others?

What do Christ's life and death mean to those who do the abusing?

This week, meditate on Isaiah 52:13–53:12. Thank God for Christ's life and death, and pray for individuals you know who need the good news of the gospel.

GOD'S UNREASONABLE MERCY

"the last will be first"

Luke 6:27-38; Matthew 20:1-16

"For this is what the high and lofty One says—
he who lives forever, whose name is holy:
I live in a high and holy place,
but also with him who is contrite and lowly in spirit,
to revive the spirit of the lowly
and to revive the heart of the contrite.
I will not accuse forever,
nor will I always be angry,
for then the spirit of man would grow faint before me—
the breath of man that I have created."
—*Isaiah 57:15-16*

In the movie, *The Mission,* a slave trader joins some Jesuit monks in order to escape prison for killing his own brother. He travels with them through jungles and over mountains, hauling behind him a large bag of heavy weapons—his own self-imposed form of penance.

When the party of Jesuits finally reaches the summit of the last mountain, the slave trader comes face to face with the child of one of the natives he formerly captured and sold to slavers. The man is struggling the last few steps, the bundle of weapons dragging him backwards, when the child approaches him, a large knife in hand. The slave trader believes that the child will kill him for what he did to the boy's father. Instead, the child cuts the man free from his huge burden, which goes tumbling down the mountainside. The slave trader is so overwhelmed by this forgiveness that he weeps and experiences a true change in his character, something the Jesuit priests had not been able to accomplish.

1. Have you ever been overwhelmed by forgiveness? Recount that experience.

Read Luke 6:27-31.

♦ **2.** What different areas of life are addressed by Jesus in this sermon?

What people in *your* life fit these categories:

enemies

those who hate you

those who speak badly of you (who curse you)

those who mistreat you

those who insult you (who slap you on the cheek)

those holding financial power over you (who ask for your coat as loan security)

those who make unmerited demands on you (who ask you to carry their burdens)

3. What seems the most difficult to you about obeying Jesus' instructions?

Read Luke 6:32-38.

4. How are Christ's followers to be different from other people?

Why should we have such a radical approach to life (verses 35-36)?

5. What are the results of mercy and forgiveness (verses 37-38)?

Read Matthew 20:1-16.

6. Why were the early workers of this story unhappy with their payment? How would you have felt if you were in their place?

Why does it seem so wrong for everyone to get the same pay, regardless of how long they worked?

♦ 7. What was Jesus really talking about in this parable (verse 1)?

8. Look at the landowner's response in verses 13-15. Has there ever been a time when God's generosity to someone else made you angry or jealous? When? When does God's ready forgiveness seem unfair to you?

9. What point is Jesus trying to make with his listeners? How is God different from us, according to this parable?

Our sense of justice and fair play was placed in us by a God who loves justice. Yet God's justice has a counterpart—mercy. Take some time to list situations in your life that require mercy—God's unreasonable, radical mercy. As you feel free to share some of these situations, pray together for God's help in being merciful.

THE DEATH OF PREJUDICE
"many parts, but one body"

1 Corinthians 12:12-26; James 2:1-9

"When one reads the major texts of church history in our modern context, an inevitable question arises: Where are the women, the people of color, the non-Westerners in the story? . . . It is a pity that historians of Christianity did not recognize long ago that a history that focuses on those with prestige and position is not the fullest reflection of our Christian heritage—in that it is out of step with how God works in the world."—**Ruth Tucker, "Colorizing Church History,"** *Christianity Today*

Favoritism and prejudice pop up in unlikely places. Church, for instance. Have you ever noticed that people with more *visible* gifts—such as musical, speaking, or teaching ability—tend to be considered more "spiritual" than those who aren't as articulate or whose personalities aren't as flamboyant? What is the general attitude in a middle-class church toward families on welfare?

Paul cuts right through to similar touchy issues in his letter to the Corinthians. People have always judged one another by faulty standards, and in this passage the apostle reminds church members of their interdependence. It is no surprise that this passage is followed by the "love chapter," 1 Corinthians 13.

1. Who do you hold in high esteem, and why?

Read 1 Corinthians 12:12-26.

2. According to verse 18, how has God arranged the parts of the human body?

3. In what sense are members of Christ's body equal? In what sense are they *not* equal?

4. If each person had the same personality and gifts as the next person, what would the result be?

5. To which parts of the body has God given greater honor (verses 24-25)? What was his purpose in doing this?

♦ **6.** What does Paul have to say about the attitude of inferiority and of superiority (verses 15-23)?

7. What causes you to feel inferior to others? What in this passage can help you deal with those feelings?

8. When are you prone to feel superior to others? What does this passage have to say to you?

9. Think of and discuss situations in which one person's suffering or rejoicing has affected other members of Christ's body.

Read James 2:1-9.

10. What does James explicitly forbid in this passage?

Why do you think he used such a specific example?

11. What is a person actually doing when he or she shows favoritism (verses 6, 9)?

12. James also points out some practical reasons that favoritism to the rich is unwise. What are they (verses 5-7)?

♦ **13.** Why is it so natural to give greater esteem to those with more power and money? Can you think of other Scripture passages that can help adjust this faulty attitude?

This week, think through the list of people you come in contact with over a month's time. What are your natural inclinations toward each of them, and why? Ask the Holy Spirit to sift through your feelings and reactions and help you deal with your own prejudices.

A RADICAL LIFESTYLE
"your light will rise in darkness"

Romans 12:2, 9-21; Colossians 3:5-17; Isaiah 58:6-12

"The Church holds out the only hope to the people of the
city. It is God's catalyst for change and regeneration. God
gave us a commission in Matthew 28:19-20, a commit-
ment in Luke 4:18-19, a prophetic calling in the book of
Amos, and examples in Jesus and Paul. From Genesis to
Revelation, the Bible is filled with urban realities and
God's intervention."—**Manuel Ortiz, "Good Neighbors:
Converting Commuter Congregations to God's Agents
in the Community,"** *Discipleship Journal*

If you ask most leaders about the major influences in their lives, they
will most often cite . . . other people. They won't talk about a certain
program or even an idea as much as they will talk about persons who
have lived the idea and made the program come alive. Similarly,
most Christians attest that they came to faith primarily through the
influence of other believers. As wonderful as books and movements

and ideologies can be, what people cry out for are tangible lives touching theirs, human contact that heals and helps. It is not surprising, then, that God chose to reach us through a person—Jesus Christ—and that he calls upon Christians to be his connection to a lost and hurting world.

1. Describe a person who has moved you to a "higher" level of life. Describe a person who has hindered your life progress and why.

Read Romans 12:2, 9-21.

2. According to verse 2, how can we escape harmful patterns of living that are so common to this world?

What else will be the result of a renewed mind?

♦ **3.** Consider for a moment popular movies, TV shows, books, and songs. Which of the character qualities in verses 9-21 are often portrayed in these forms of media? Which are rarely or never portrayed?

Which quality—to you—seems the most out of place in our society and why?

4. How can we, in daily life, "honor one another above ourselves" (verse 10)? What does it mean to be *devoted* to someone?

5. How would you define *hospitality?*

6. What do you do to "keep your spiritual fervor," as we are instructed in verse 11?

7. How are God's people to go through affliction?

Read Colossians 3:5-17.

8. Why is it so important for us to put off our old ways and put on new ones?

9. What practical suggestions are given for implementing our new lifestyle?

Read Isaiah 58:6-12.

♦ **10.** Throughout history, people have often fasted and prayed in order to get God's attention. What does *God* say will get his attention (verses 6-7)?

What will be the result of those actions?

♦ **11.** Explain what you think these phrases mean:

"your light will break forth like the dawn" (verse 8)

"your light will rise in the darkness" (verse 10)

"you will be like a well-watered garden" (verse 11)

12. In verse 12, Isaiah is referring to the ruins of the nation Israel—both physical and spiritual. How can this verse apply to God's people today?

The passages of this study are about a lifestyle that is different and about being an example. How is your life an example to others? How is it different from what people expect of a "normal" person?

OUR HOPE AND PROMISE
"arise, Lord!"

Psalm 37

"Why does the wicked man revile God?
Why does he say to himself,
'He won't call me to account'?
But you, O God, do see trouble and grief;
you consider it to take it in hand.
The victim commits himself to you;
you are the helper of the fatherless."
—*Psalm 10:13-14*

The world feels more unsafe and more unfair every day. It is a wearying thing just to live decently, minding one's own business. But as believers in Christ, we have much more to do than merely survive, and we have much more to hope for than some peace and quiet in the here and now. *Sojourners* editor Jim Wallis put it quite well in his December 1992 column: "To steadfastly put our trust in the gospel is to boldly proclaim that the violence, oppression, and chaos will not have the last word."

1. If a person were to ask you what difference it made in today's world to be a Christian, what would you say?

Read Psalm 37.

2. The "wicked" and "evil" are referred to numerous times in this chapter. List the activities and attitudes that characterize them.

3. How do the "righteous," "blameless," and "meek" differ from the wicked?

◆ **4.** In what ways is this psalm *realistic* about life; what kinds of situations does the psalmist acknowledge go on, even though they are not good?

5. In the face of injustice and cruelty, why are we told *not* to be overwhelmed and discouraged?

6. What will become of the wicked?

7. The psalmist was well acquainted with the attitudes we are tempted to fall into and the actions we want to take in times of distress and oppression. In the following verses, what are we encouraged to do and *not* to do? If there is a corresponding reason or consequence mentioned, list it also.

verses 1-2

verses 3-4

verses 5-6

verse 7

verse 8

verse 27

verse 34

verse 37

8. Who will take ultimate action in the world and make all things as they should be?

♦ **9.** What kinds of help does God give us while we are in bad situations?

10. What must we do, in simple terms, in order to be rescued from the evil in this world (verse 40)?

11. How can a Christian "take refuge in God" today?

12. What do you do in painful or unjust situations?

Spend some time as a group writing a "Justice Statement." This statement should include:

The Christian definition of justice
The Christian definition of mercy
Why it is possible for Christians to live out these definitions
Why the Christian life should demonstrate hope for the world

LEADER'S NOTES

■ **Study 1/What God Requires**

Question 6. Examples of the prudent being silenced are not hard to find. Products continue to be approved when studies done independently of their producers indicate questions about safety or effectiveness. After the space shuttle, *Challenger,* exploded, killing all of its crew, it was discovered that some people at NASA had questioned the safety of certain parts of the spacecraft, yet the reports had never reached the top of the organizational hierarchy and thus were not addressed. Usually the bigger the organization, the more pressure to be silent is put on people who attempt to be honest, whether in mundane office politics or matters of public concern.

■ **Study 2/For Those Who Lead**

Question 2. Sadly, even the better kings of Israel neglected these instructions. King David had tremendous material resources; possibly it was guilt over this that made him so intent on building a temple for God, for he says in 2 Samuel 7:2, "Here I am, living in a palace of cedar, while the ark of God remains in a tent." His son

Solomon "was greater in riches . . . than all the other kings of the earth" (1 Kings 10:23); his riches are catalogued in great detail in 1 Kings 10:14-29. He also "loved many foreign women," having "seven hundred wives of royal birth and three hundred concubines, and his wives led him astray" (1 Kings 11:1, 3).

Question 5. Prophets "received a specific and personal call from God." They came into God's presence and then relayed to the people what counsel they had received from the Lord. "Alone of the nations of antiquity, Israel had a true awareness of history. They owed it to the prophets . . ." Because of the prophets, God's people could know the meaning of events even before they happened.

Often, prophets confronted rulers and entire nations with the true view of a holy God. It was "only the false prophet who dared to take the office upon himself," and obviously many self-proclaimed prophets were telling the people what they wanted to hear *(The New Bible Dictionary,* Second Edition, p. 975. Wheaton, Ill.: Tyndale House Publishers, Inc., 1982).

■ Study 3/For Those Who Follow

Question 12. We prove that we know Christ. See 1 John 3:16-28. This is also in agreement with James' teaching about faith and works.

■ Study 4/The Place of Power

Question 3. Naboth was adhering to Levitical law concerning tribal property. See Leviticus 25:23. Were it not for answering to that higher authority (God's law), Naboth would have nothing to gain by refusing a king's request. He no doubt would have received ample money or land in compensation.

Question 9. Elijah has long been a thorn in Ahab's side. See 1 Kings 18:16-46 and 20:13-43.

Question 10. For a king or queen (or anyone, for that matter) to go without proper burial was the ultimate disgrace. Enemies would sometimes scatter the remains of those they conquered, or they would display the bodies of leaders, hung from walls and trees, to desecrate their names and tribes.

Question 11. These judgments did come to pass in 1 Kings 22. Although God had mercy on Ahab, Ahab did not learn from his mistakes.

Question 13. "Throughout the Bible, *cup* is used figuratively as containing the share of blessings or disasters alloted to a man or nation or his divinely appointed fate" *(New Bible Dictionary,* Second Edition, p. 255).

Although baptism generally symbolizes repentance and change of life, it is also an initiation, of sorts, into a new position (for Christians, into the body of Christ) and therefore new requirements and responsibilities.

■ **Study 5/Wealth and Complacency**

Question 4. In the Bible, God's nation is often referred to by the name of a prominent ancestor, such as Abraham, Jacob, or Joseph. Thus, Amos refers to the ruin of the *nation* when he says "the ruin of Joseph."

Question 7. "Amen," "ruler of God's creation" refers to Jesus Christ. This passage is a letter from God to the church of Laodicea. The book of Revelation has been interpreted in a variety of ways according to the different methods of interpreting visionary and prophetic passages.

Whether this letter was meant for the actual church of Laodicea (there was a church in that city), or for all the churches of a particular historical age, the message of these verses is not at all ambiguous; sins are clearly identified, as well as God's view of them.

Question 10. One of Jesus' four temptations in the wilderness was for wealth and power (see Luke 4:5-8). Many times during his ministry he could have "cashed in" on a circuit of sensational miracle making and could have enjoyed great prestige and adoration (see John 6:14-15). Yet, he saw the real needs of people—for health in body, soul, mind, and spirit, and preferred to deal with those areas of desperation and sin.

■ Study 6/Down with Oppression!

Question 3. Most of us can't even relate to the day-to-day confusion that fills the lives of the oppressed. For example, in America's history, Negro slaves never knew when their families would be split apart, who they would be sold to and where they would relocate, or what kind of discipline their masters would employ. The women didn't know if or when they would be raped and impregnated by their masters and what would become of those children. They had no idea what kind of care they would receive when they were sick or injured. They usually didn't understand the unspoken rules of the house until they had already trespassed one of them. There is no real rest for people in such circumstances; extreme emotional stress is constant.

Question 6. Other Scriptures that relate human activity to the welfare of creation are Genesis 3:17-19, and Romans 8:18-25. For further study of this subject, read the NetWork Discussion Guide *Tending Creation* (1991) and *While Creation Waits* (1992) by Dale and Sandy Larsen (Wheaton, Ill.: Harold Shaw Publishers).

■ Study 7/Balance of Wealth

Question 5. In such a system, a family could go only so far down the spiral of poverty, and they would always have the comfort of knowing that at Jubilee their children or grandchildren would be able to recover from the family's present losses. Thus, hopelessness and despair would not figure in so prominently during times of financial hardship.

By the same token, no one person or family would have the opportunity to amass great fortunes or build personal empires that would eventually sap resources from other tribes. People could have the satisfaction of making wealth for themselves and living well—but only a few decades at a time. The same system that saved others from hopelessness could prevent arrogance in the more fortunate.

Question 8. Another passage that deals with economic policy is Deuteronomy 15:1-11; God's people are commanded to cancel all debts every seven years.

Question 9. Put in very general terms, communism does not allow for autonomy; people receive allotments and do not have the freedom to develop their own financial picture. Also, communist systems require that resources go to a common coffer, which is often controlled by a few "leaders." The people of Israel were given freedom in how they used their land, crops, and homes.

Capitalism allows much freedom but rarely implements effective safeguards against abuses. In a capitalistic system *without* safeguards, the wealthy become increasingly rich and powerful, and the poor are allowed to remain poor from generation to generation, without much hope of recovery. A few powerful people or organizations are able to gain disproportionate control over the lives of others, and eventually everything in the economic system serves the needs of a very small portion of the population.

Question 10. In Paul's letter to Timothy (1 Timothy 5:3-8), further guidelines were set up that distinguished between those widows who were truly in need and those who had resources or who still had family members to help care for them. The church's generosity was to be tempered with good judgment and discretion.

■ Study 8/Our Response to the Poor

Question 5. To be sold to non-Jews meant a loss not only of personal freedom, but of culture and religion. The surrounding cultures did not worship the God of Israel; their entire moral systems were different. Slaves were also more likely to be treated harshly by owners who were not of their own nation or tribe.

Question 9. There's a big difference between a debtor going into his own home and willingly handing over his collateral, and his creditor coming into his home and seizing the property. This is an issue of self-respect and privacy—important aspects of emotional and spiritual health. No other explanation is given for this particular point of the law. Such a stipulation would also prevent a creditor from entering a home and taking a few other items he happened to see, besides the collateral that had been agreed upon.

Question 10. Today, others besides widows and orphans could be named in special categories of need, such as single mothers and those struggling with mental and/or physical disabilities. Many such people have no extended family into which they can be absorbed and cared for. Israel's tribal communities were the welfare system of the day, yet some people fell through the cracks, such as elderly widows with no living sons. Today's welfare systems still miss a large number of people who have legitimate needs.

Question 12. The New Testament church followed Old Testament principle and was a giving church, but there were also policies toward *work* that helped keep church life and giving in balance. To study further, read 2 Thessalonians 3:6-15.

■ Study 9/Why Christ Came

Question 5. "These verses were quoted in Matthew 12:18-21 with reference to Christ, the Chosen One. The Chosen One reveals a character of gentleness, encouragement, justice, and truth. When you feel broken and bruised, or burned out in your spiritual life, God won't step on you or toss you aside as useless, but he will gently pick you up. God's loving attributes are desperately needed by mankind today. We can show such sensitivity through God's Spirit to people around us, reflecting God's goodness and honesty to them" *(Life Application Bible,* p. 1028. Wheaton, Ill.: Tyndale House Publishers, 1988).

Question 8. "Anointed" in Israel's literature meant to be chosen by God for a special task. In the Old Testament, a person anointed was given the Holy Spirit in order to perform that task. Remember that this was before the Spirit was given to dwell in the lives of believers.

■ Study 10/God's Unreasonable Mercy

Question 2. These categories need not apply only to *individuals;* there is plenty of conflict between political parties and racial groups.

Question 7. Jesus was not advocating inequitable payment systems in the actual work world. James 5:4 condemns unfair payment practices. But he used a very common situation to drive home how different God's ideas of fairness and mercy are from the world's ideas. The story was so ridiculous that it was bound to get the listeners' attention and show them that God's forgiveness and acceptance happen quite apart from any of our own work or "earning."

▓ Study 11/The Death of Prejudice

Question 6. It is no coincidence that Paul speaks of spiritual gifts in one breath and attitudes of superiority/inferiority in the next. Although the Spirit gives us gifts for the purpose of serving one another (1 Peter 4:10), this focus is often lost when Christians follow the world's example of making comparisons. "Gifts are for building up the entire church, not for making one person feel proud and another feel left out. Paul listed several gifts, but there is no reason to suppose these lists are comprehensive. He did not mention gifts which are widely recognized today, such as gifts of music, of youth work, or of counseling. Whatever skill you have which can be used to serve Christ and His people is a gift of the Spirit. Gifts may be given suddenly or developed slowly" *(Disciple's Study Bible* [NIV], p. 1462. Nashville: Holman Bible Publishers, 1988).

Question 13. We are warned numerous times in Scripture not to be taken in by the allure of riches or spend our energy courting the favor of rich people. For instance, it is foolish to enjoy too much the food at a ruler's table or that of a stingy person (Proverbs 23:1-8), because there is usually another agenda on the minds of such people. That same passage warns us not to make riches our goal in life. Other verses reminding us of the deceitfulness and oppression that often come with wealth and power are: Proverbs 11:28; 22:7; 28:11, 22; 30:8; Jeremiah 9:23; Micah 6:10-12; 1 Timothy 6:6-10.

■ Study 12/A Radical Lifestyle

Question 3. In this passage, Paul is giving instructions for the Christian life through positive statements—telling what we must *do*. For a very similar set of instructions stated in a "do not" form, turn to Leviticus 19:9-18.

Question 10. God refers to fasting in this passage because the people made a big show of religious fasts and observances, thinking such activities gave them credibility before God and that God would therefore do what they wanted.

Question 11. God's people are referred to as light in other Scriptures. See Matthew 5:14-16; Ephesians 5:8-10; Philippians 2:14-15; and 1 Thessalonians 5:5.

■ Study 13/Our Hope and Promise

Question 4. The Bible has never downplayed reality. This psalm cites many instances in which cruelty and injustice do prevail; the tone of the writer, however, conveys that life will not always be so.

Christians who are unaccustomed to suffering (including many of us in the United States and Western Europe) have allowed the Gospel to be diluted, preaching a "health and wealth" message that can only apply to those who are unoppressed and relatively wealthy. If an *honest* reading of Psalm 37 and other such passages causes some confusion or discomfort, it is because our prevailing culture has allowed us to ignore the harsher elements of the Christian experience—such as suffering, persecution, and perseverance.

Question 9. Many other passages from the book of Psalms speak of how God helps us during times of pain, darkness, and persecution; for those members of the group who are suffering, a program for reading through Psalms could be helpful. Also, the book of Acts outlines Paul's life of ups and downs—a down-to-earth, yet inspirational life story. 2 Corinthians 6:3-10 is encouraging, especially for those who suffer because they maintain a lifestyle of ministry to others.

WHAT SHOULD WE STUDY NEXT?

To help your group answer that question, we've listed the Fisherman Guides by category so you can choose your next study.

TOPICAL STUDIES

Angels, Wright

Becoming Women of Purpose, Barton

Building Your House on the Lord, Brestin

Discipleship, Reapsome

Doing Justice, Showing Mercy, Wright

Encouraging Others, Johnson

Examining the Claims of Jesus, Brestin

Friendship, Brestin

The Fruit of the Spirit, Briscoe

Great Doctrines of the Bible, Board

Great Passages of the Bible, Plueddemann

Great Prayers of the Bible, Plueddemann

Growing Through Life's Challenges, Reapsome

Guidance & God's Will, Stark

Heart Renewal, Goring

Higher Ground, Brestin

Lifestyle Priorities, White

Marriage, Stevens

Miracles, Castleman

Moneywise, Larsen

One Body, One Spirit, Larsen

The Parables of Jesus, Hunt

Prayer, Jones

The Prophets, Wright

Proverbs & Parables, Brestin

Satisfying Work, Stevens & Schoberg

Senior Saints, Reapsome

Sermon on the Mount, Hunt

Spiritual Warfare, Moreau

The Ten Commandments, Briscoe

Who Is God? Seemuth

Who Is the Holy Spirit? Knuckles & Van Reken

Who Is Jesus? Van Reken

Witnesses to All the World, Plueddemann

Worship, Sibley

BIBLE BOOK STUDIES

Genesis, Fromer & Keyes

Job, Klug

Psalms, Klug

Proverbs: Wisdom That Works, Wright

Ecclesiastes, Brestin

Jonah, Habakkuk, & Malachi, Fromer & Keyes

Matthew, Sibley

Mark, Christensen

Luke, Keyes

John: Living Word, Kuniholm

Acts 1-12, Christensen

Paul (Acts 13-28), Christensen

Romans: The Christian Story, Reapsome

1 Corinthians, Hummel

Strengthened to Serve (2 Corinthians), Plueddemann

Galatians, Titus & Philemon, Kuniholm

Ephesians, Baylis

Philippians, Klug

Colossians, Shaw

Letters to the Thessalonians, Fromer & Keyes

Letters to Timothy, Fromer & Keyes

Hebrews, Hunt

James, Christensen

1 & 2 Peter, Jude, Brestin

How Should a Christian Live? (1, 2 & 3 John), Brestin

Revelation, Hunt

BIBLE CHARACTER STUDIES

David: Man after God's Own Heart, Castleman

Elijah, Castleman

Great People of the Bible, Plueddemann

King David: Trusting God for a Lifetime, Castleman

Men Like Us, Heidebrecht & Scheuermann

Paul (Acts 13-28), Christensen

Peter, Castleman

Ruth & Daniel, Stokes

Women Like Us, Barton

Women Who Achieved for God, Christensen

Women Who Believed God, Christensen